# Plants of the World

## Claire Llewellyn

Smart Apple Media

This book has been published in cooperation with Franklin Watts.

Editor: Jennifer Schofield, Consultant: Caroline Boisset, Art director: Jonathan Hair, Design: Susi Martin, Picture researcher: Diana Morris, Photography: Ray Moller, unless otherwise acknowledged, Artwork: Ian Thompson

Acknowledgements:
Stuart Baines/Ecoscene: 17. Andy Binns/Ecoscene: 10. Tony Wilson-Bligh/Ecoscene: 20. Garry Braasch/Corbis: 23t. Andrew Brown/Ecoscene: 29bl. Phillip Colla/Ecoscene: 25. Anthony Cooper/Ecoscene: 8, 12. Stephen Coynes/Ecoscene: 29br. Simon Grove/Ecoscene: 27. Eric & David Hosking/Corbis: 11. Patrick Johns/Corbis: 3, 29c. Sally Morgan/Ecoscene: front cover, 18. Fritz Polking/Ecoscene: 13, 29bc, 29cr. Promeck Services/Ecoscene: 14. Kjell Sandved/Ecoscene: 19, 23b. Scott T. Smith/Corbis: 24. Gabriela Staebler/zefa/Corbis: 21. Paul Thompson/Ecoscene: 7. Watts Publishing: 26, 29cl.

Published in the United States by Smart Apple Media
2140 Howard Drive West, North Mankato, Minnesota 56003

Library of Congress Cataloging-in-Publication Data

Llewellyn, Claire.
Plants of the world / by Claire Llewellyn.
p. cm.—(Understanding plants)
Includes bibliographical references and index.
ISBN-13: 978-1-59920-032-3
1. Plants—Juvenile literature. I. Title.


QK49.L74 2007
580—dc22    2006027605

9 8 7 6 5 4 3 2 1

# Contents

# Habitats of the world

Plants can be found almost everywhere on Earth—on snow-topped mountains and in low-lying swamps, in deserts and in the sea. They have adapted to survive in almost every kind of habitat and climate.

## Different climates

There are three main climate zones in the world: the polar zone, which lies close to the Poles; the tropical zone, which lies near the equator; and the temperate zone, which lies in between the two. These main zones can be divided into smaller areas. For example, the tropical zone includes rain forest, desert, and grassland, each of which has its own particular pattern of temperature and rainfall. Some climates provide warmth, light, and reasonable rainfall—everything a plant needs to grow well. Other climate zones include long periods of cold, darkness, and drought, and are more difficult places for plants to grow.

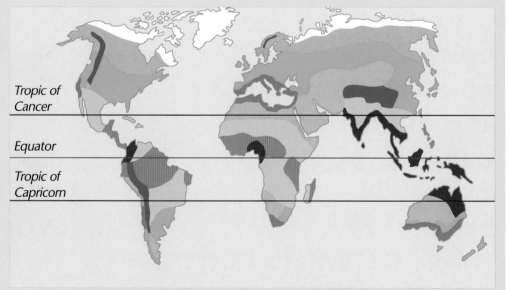

Tropic of Cancer

Equator

Tropic of Capricorn

*Earth's main climate zones can be divided into smaller zones. The climate and landscape of each area affect the plants that grow there.*

Temperate

Rain forest

Desert

Mountain

Coniferous forest

Grassland

Tundra

Mediterranean

Monsoon

# Different environments

Plants are the oldest forms of life. They have lived on Earth for about 420 million years, and during this time, they have evolved into a huge and diverse group. For example, there is not just a single species of pine tree; there are more than 100 different species, and each one is unique. Scientists have not yet identified every plant in the world, but they estimate that there are probably about 400,000 different kinds.

## Get this!

The only place on Earth that plants cannot grow is the South Pole. It is too dark and too cold, and it is covered in ice, a form of water that plants cannot use.

## Adaptation and diversity

Plants have lived on Earth for millions of years. During this time, different species have adapted the way they grow to help them survive in particular habitats. This process has resulted in the plant kingdom's huge diversity. From conifers to cacti and poppies to palms, this book looks at some of the world's plant species and the many places they have managed to inhabit.

*Coconut palms have adapted to grow in tropical regions, particularly on tropical islands. Their slender trunks are strong enough to withstand hurricane-force winds, and their fruit— the coconut—is so buoyant that it can float on water and sprout on distant shores.*

# How plants grow

Plants can live in many different places because they have simple needs. To grow well, they require sunlight, warmth, water, and nutrients from the soil.

## The parts of a plant

Most plants are made up of the same basic parts. They have a system of roots below the ground and a stem with stalks and leaves above the ground. Many plants also have flowers, which help them grow seeds and reproduce themselves. Each part of a plant has its own job to do, but it also works with all the other parts to help the plant grow and be healthy.

## PARTS OF A PLANT

**Stem**
*The stem holds the plant up to the light. It contains tubes that carry food and water around the plant.*

**Flower**
*This contains the male and female parts of a plant. They help it produce seeds.*

**Leaves**
*The leaves absorb sunlight and make food for the plant.*

**Roots**
*The roots anchor the plant in the soil. They also suck up water and nutrients.*

*Like all plants, grass needs water to grow. In periods of hot, dry weather, water sprinklers are often used to keep grass green and healthy.*

## Plants need light

Plants need food to grow. Unlike animals, which have to find or hunt for food, plants can make their food inside their leaves by a process called photosynthesis. To do this, plants need plenty of light. They use the energy from sunlight, water from the soil, and a gas called carbon dioxide from the air to produce sugary substances called carbohydrates. The carbohydrates give plants the energy to live and grow.

## THE PROCESS OF PHOTOSYNTHESIS

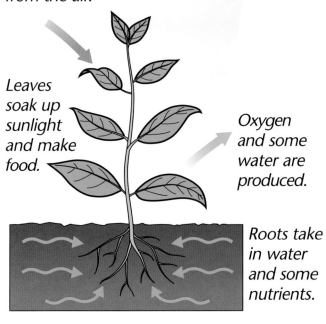

Carbon dioxide enters the leaves from the air.

Leaves soak up sunlight and make food.

Oxygen and some water are produced.

Roots take in water and some nutrients.

## Other needs

Along with light, plants need water. Without water, plants do not grow as quickly, and often they will wilt and die. Plants also need nutrients that are found in the soil. This keeps plants green and healthy. Some warmth is also important for plants. Warmth encourages seeds to sprout and speeds the growing process. Plants grow quicker in warm conditions, and they slow down when it is cold.

# Plants in the tundra

Dark, windy, and cold for much of the year, the tundra is a challenging habitat for plants. However, there are some species that grow successfully here because of special adaptations that help them survive.

## What's this?

This low bush has small, round, blue-black berries that are sweet and good to eat.

## A harsh climate

To the far north of Asia, Europe, and North America lies a vast, barren land. This uninhabited wilderness is called the "tundra," a Finnish word meaning "treeless." The climate in the tundra is cold and harsh with strong, biting winds. The winter months are long and dark, with an average temperature of about –68 °F (–20 °C). Summers in the tundra are cool and brief with long hours of daylight. The ground is covered by snow for much of the year. The top layer of the soil thaws out in summer, but lower layers are permanently frozen.

*No trees grow in the tundra, but low-growing plants have adapted to survive the cold climate.*

# Out of the wind

Plants can only survive in the tundra if they can keep out of the savage wind. Heathers and mosses grow in low, dense clusters or cushions. These trap moisture in the center, preventing the plants from drying out. Most trees cannot grow in the tundra because they would be flattened by the wind. However, the Arctic willow has adapted in a special way. Instead of growing up, it grows close to the ground and is rarely more than 4 inches (10 cm) high.

*The Arctic willow grows long, thin clusters of tiny, petal-less flowers called catkins.*

## Get this!

Conditions in the tundra are cold and bleak, but it is still a suitable habitat for more than 1,700 different kinds of plants.

## The race to survive

The tundra climate is so cold that most plants grow very slowly. However, the 500 species of wildflowers that grow in the tundra have adapted in a different way. As soon as the snow melts in spring, seeds from the previous year germinate, and the seedlings grow very quickly. The young plants produce buds and flowers, which rapidly develop seeds. In a matter of weeks, the ripe seeds fall to the ground, ready to survive the long, cold winter until spring returns again.

# A coniferous forest

In the far north, to the south of the tundra, lies a great, dark carpet of coniferous trees. This forest is home to few plant species, but each one grows in huge numbers and succeeds in surviving the cold.

## A long winter

Although the forests lie south of the tundra, the climate here is still a harsh one. The summers are warmer than in the tundra, but the winters are long, with heavy snow and freezing winds. During the cold months, the ground is like an iceberg and plants are starved for water. In spring, winter's grip begins to loosen, and the top layer of the soil begins to thaw.

## Get this!

The world's largest forest region is the huge coniferous forest that stretches 7,500 miles (12,000 km) across the north of Russia. It is known as the taiga.

*Coniferous trees form huge, dense forests in the far north. Little snow settles on the trees compared with that on the ground.*

## Adapted to the cold

The plants best adapted to this climate are coniferous trees such as spruce and pine. They have a small, needle-shaped leaf, whose tough, waxy coat is resistant to frost and locks in the trees' precious water. The trees, most of which are evergreen, shed their leaves slowly throughout the year instead of losing them all at once. This helps the trees conserve energy and absorb sunlight throughout the year.

## Seeds and cones

Unlike other kinds of plants, conifers do not produce flowers. Instead, the male and female parts of the plant develop in separate woody cones. The small male cones produce a yellow dust called pollen, which is spread by the wind. If pollen grains land on the larger female cones, they can begin to make seeds. The seeds grow slowly over two to three years. When they are ripe, the cones' scales open and the seeds float to the ground.

## CONIFEROUS TREES

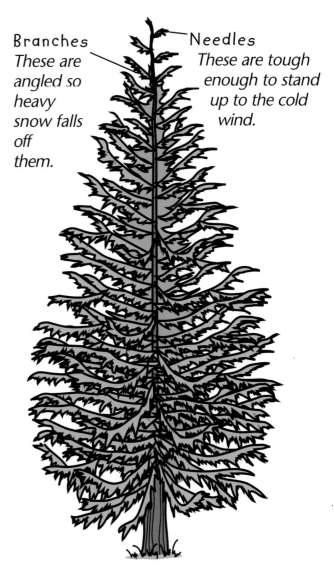

Branches
*These are angled so heavy snow falls off them.*

Needles
*These are tough enough to stand up to the cold wind.*

# Try this!

Cones can be used to forecast the weather. In damp weather, they close their scales to protect their seeds; in dry weather, they open them again. Find a cone and test this theory. Are there any seeds inside your cone?

# Mountain plants

Mountains are found all over the world and in all the different climate zones. There are several different "climates" on a mountain itself. Plant species that grow on the lower slopes cannot survive at the top.

## A mountain climate

A mountain climate is very changeable with large differences in temperature between the day and night. Though lower valleys may be reasonably sheltered, at the peak there are freezing temperatures and strong winds. Summers here are short, but there is plenty of strong sunlight throughout the year. The sun, wind, and freezing temperatures make mountains a very dry habitat for plants.

## What's this?

This plant grows high in the mountains. It has a white, felt-like flower and hairy leaves that act like a warm coat.

*High up, flowers are usually large and bright. This helps attract insects, which are scarce on mountains, to pollinate the flowers.*

# Vegetation zones

The plants change as you climb up a mountain. The Alps are a temperate mountain range. In the foothills of the Alps, there is a wide variety of deciduous trees. Higher up, as the air gets colder, conifers begin to take over. Higher still, the trees die out and there are meadows with grasses and wild flowers. Few plants can survive at the very top, but there are some small plants called alpines.

## LIFE ON A MOUNTAIN

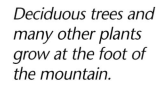

*Some plants, such as alpines, grow at the top. They have adapted to the cold.*

*Trees die on the higher slopes. Grasses and wild flowers grow here.*

*Coniferous forests grow high up where the air is cold.*

*Deciduous trees and many other plants grow at the foot of the mountain.*

## Looking at alpines

Alpines have adapted to the harsh conditions of mountain life. These plants grow in low cushions to keep out of the wind. Many of them, such as the edelweiss, also have furry leaves and flowers, which trap heat and help prevent water loss.

Because they live in a dry habitat, many alpines also have long roots to suck up water from deep underground. The plants reproduce quickly in the short growing season. In late spring, as soon as the ice melts, the plants burst into flower and set seed before the first snow in fall.

# In the temperate zone

Life in the temperate zone follows a seasonal pattern. For most of the year, plants get a good balance of light, water, and warmth, but many have adapted in a special way to survive the winter cold.

## A temperate climate

In the temperate regions of the world, there are four distinct seasons in the year. In spring the days grow longer and brighter. In summer the days are long and warm. The days become shorter and cooler in fall, and in winter the days are short and dark, while the weather is cold and frosty. Plants are living things—they sense these changes and adapt the way they grow. Deciduous trees grow particularly well in a temperate climate. These trees are usually broadleaved, and they lose their leaves in fall.

## What's this?

This tree's large leaves turn a spectacular red in fall. It has a sweet sap that can be used to make syrup.

## BUDS ON DECIDUOUS TREES

*In winter, the leaf buds are protected by scales.*

*In early spring, the scales open.*

*The buds burst open and the leaves start to grow.*

## Try this!

In fall or winter, look closely at some trees. You should see next year's buds on the branches. If possible, feel the buds. How are they protected from the winter weather?

# Looking at trees

In spring, the deciduous trees' long roots suck up water and the trees grow very quickly. On every branch, broad, flat leaves unfold and stretch out in the sunshine, forming a dense canopy that soaks up light. This provides energy for the tree to grow and to produce flowers, fruits, and seeds. As the days shorten in fall, there is not enough light to make food for the tree. The leaves dry out and fall to the ground. The tree stops growing and rests until spring.

# Try this!

Compare a deciduous and a coniferous tree: look at their height, shape, branches, and leaves, as well as their cones, fruits, and seeds. How are the trees different? How are they the same?

*Many woodland plants flower early in the season while they can make use of the sun's rays. Once all the leaf buds on the trees open, the plants will be in the shade.*

# Under the trees

The leaves that fall from deciduous trees rot down on the ground. The nutrients they contain mix with the soil and help fertilize it. Other plants that grow on the woodland floor benefit from this. Some of them, such as woodland flowers, have adapted to the trees' seasonal growth. In early spring, before the trees have leaves, they use the energy from the available light to flower and set seed.

17

# Desert plants

Deserts are very dry places with poor soil and scarce and unreliable rainfall. They are one of the most difficult habitats for plants to grow in. Yet some species have adapted to the conditions and manage to survive.

## A hostile environment

Deserts receive less than 10 inches (25 cm) of rainfall a year. The rain does not fall evenly every year—for example, one year there may be no rain, but the next it may all come in one tremendous storm. Temperatures in deserts are very extreme: at midday the air may be a scorching 122 °F (50 °C), while at night it may dip to near freezing. The ground is inhospitable, too. It is covered with bare rock, pebbles, gravel, or sand that blows around in the wind.

## Storing water

Plants cannot live without water, but some, known as succulents, have adapted to survive on very little. Cacti are succulents. They collect as much rainwater as they can through a network of roots near the surface of the ground. They store the water in their tough, pulpy stems, which have a thick, waxy surface to prevent the water from evaporating. Many desert plants are covered in sharp spines that protect them from thirsty animals.

*This barrel cactus is found in the Sonoran desert in the United States. It stores water in its pulpy stem, which is pleated like an accordian, so it can pump up quickly after rain.*

## Surviving as seed

Other plants have adapted to desert conditions in a different way. Instead of living from one season to another, some plants live and die in a single season and survive periods of drought as seeds. When it rains, the seeds germinate and grow quickly. In the following few weeks, they produce leaves, flowers, and seeds, which are spread by the desert wind. The parent plants then wither and die, but their seeds survive until it rains again.

*Pebble plants have adapted to desert conditions by storing water in their leaves and growing partly underground. The plants are camouflaged to look like stones. This protects them from being eaten by gerbils, tortoises, and other desert animals.*

## Get this!

Desert peoples have always relied on plants. The Bushmen of the Kalahari dig up swollen roots, known as *bi*, for their life-saving stores of water.

## What's this?

This tall tree grows in deserts, in green places called oases. The trees produce an edible brown fruit, which is very sweet and sticky when dried.

# Tropical grasslands

In some parts of the world, the weather is hot and dry for much of the year, but there is also a season of rain. These places are perfect for grasses. They grow green and tall in the wet season and die when it is dry.

## How grasses grow

Grasses are tough flowering plants. They have roots, stems, and leaves like other plants, but they grow in a different way. Their stems grow horizontally along the ground. Buds on the stems put out shoots that grow into long, narrow leaves called blades. Grass plants produce a mass of stringy roots that bind the soil into a tough mat. When it rains, the roots suck up water from the soil before it can sink under ground.

## Try this!

Take a close look at some grass. Can you see the horizontal stems? Now tug the grass and try to pull it up. This is very hard to do because of the way the roots bind with the soil.

*A herd of wildebeest crosses the savanna. The animals depend on grasses for food, and when the plants wither in the dry season, wildebeest migrate across the African plains in search of fresh grazing.*

# Tough survivors

The tropical grasslands of eastern Africa are known as the savanna. They provide food for the huge herds of wildebeest, zebra, and other herbivores that feed on the blades of grass. Grazing would destroy most other plants, but grasses can recover quickly because the new shoots grow at ground level rather than higher up the plant. The grasses also survive the regular fires caused by lightning strikes. While the tall, dry blades burn in the fire, the horizontal stems remain unharmed and shoot up the next time it rains.

## What's this?

This curious tree is sometimes called an upside-down tree. It grows on the savanna and stores water in its trunk. After the rains, the trunk is fat but shrinks in times of drought.

# The acacia tree

In the parts of the grasslands where more rain falls, acacia trees grow. Like grass, they have adapted to survive drought, fire, and hungry animals. Their long taproots reach water underground and, if the plant is burned by fire, can produce new shoots. Acacias keep most animals at bay with their long, sharp thorns. Large ants make their homes in the thorns and help protect the tree by biting any animals that feed on its leaves.

*The acacia tree has adapted to its dry habitat by growing very small leaves. Yet its spreading, umbrella-like shape still allows it to capture plenty of sunlight for photosynthesis.*

# Tropical rain forests

A rain forest climate provides plants with sunlight, warmth, and water—everything they need to grow well. That is why there are more plant species in these remarkable forests than in any other kind of habitat.

## A tropical climate

The weather hardly changes in a tropical climate. Every day there is plenty of strong, warm sunshine and a heavy shower of rain. The temperature is warm both day and night. There are no frosts, no droughts, no months of darkness. The air is always moist and sticky, providing perfect conditions for plants.

## Soaring tall

So many plants grow in a rain forest that they compete with each other for the light. Trees have adapted to win the contest by having tall, straight trunks that soar upward with no side branches to slow them down. At the top, the trees spread out to form a dense canopy that produces leaves, flowers, and fruits. Tall trees need a lot of support, so rain forest trees grow huge buttress roots, which can be up to 15 feet tall. They snake out above the surface of the ground and provide extra strength at the base of the trees.

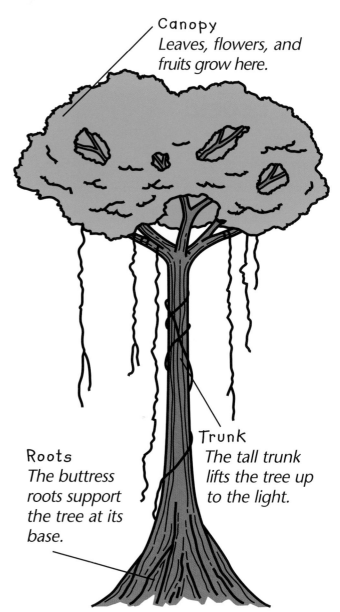

A RAIN FOREST TREE

**Canopy**
*Leaves, flowers, and fruits grow here.*

**Trunk**
*The tall trunk lifts the tree up to the light.*

**Roots**
*The buttress roots support the tree at its base.*

## A lift to the light

Rain forest trees cast a deep shade on the forest floor. Plants such as ferns grow well here and have adapted to the gloom. Others use the trees to get a lift up to the light. One group of plants, known as epiphytes, has adapted to live high up in the trees. Its seeds are blown onto the bark, where they sprout and grow. The bromeliad plant is an epiphyte. Its rosette shape channels rainwater into the center of the plant, where it forms a pool of water. This provides the plant with the moisture and nutrients that other plants obtain through their roots.

## What's this?

This tropical tree is grown in plantations and is tapped for a sticky, milky juice called latex, which can be used to make boots and tires.

## Get this!

Rain forest plants are extraordinarily diverse. There are about 18,000 different kinds of orchids. Many tropical orchids live by perching on other plants.

# Plants in the ocean

The only plants that can live in the sea belong to a plant family called algae. Algae are the oldest and simplest kind of plants. Most of them are very tiny, but some, such as seaweeds, are larger and form "forests" in the sea.

A mass of seaweed cloaks the rocks along this shoreline at low tide. The plants do not have proper roots; instead, they have a "foot" called a holdfast that anchors them to rocks.

## Sea and shore

With its deep, salty water and pounding waves, the sea is a difficult place for plants to grow. However, for those plants that can survive in salt water, there is plenty of light near the surface and reasonable warmth. The sea is also rich in nutrients provided by decaying animals on the seabed. Along the coast, plants face a special challenge. Twice a day the tide goes out, and plants that grow there risk drying out. Seaweeds are the largest kind of algae. They are covered with a slimy coating that keeps them from drying out when the tide is low.

## Get this!

Seaweeds contain such useful nutrients that we harvest them and use them to make fertilizer.

## Seaweeds

These sea plants have adapted to the ocean by having strong, rubbery stems called fronds. The fronds are flexible and can ride the waves. Some species of seaweed have air-filled pockets called bladders, which help keep their fronds afloat, allowing them to absorb light and make food for the plant. One kind of seaweed, known as kelp, grows fronds as tall as any rain forest tree, creating thick "forests" under the sea.

*Sea plants need to be able to reach the light to make food. To do this, seaweed has air bladders that keep the fronds afloat and within reach of the sunlight.*

## Try this!

Next time you are at the seaside, take home a piece of seaweed. Let it dry for a day or so, then put it back in water. What happens? Now leave it out of water for longer periods. How long can it survive?

## The soup of the sea

Smaller kinds of algae float freely in the water. Masses of these microscopic algae float on the surface of the ocean, absorbing the available sunlight. Known collectively as phytoplankton, the algae reproduce every few hours simply by splitting in two. This creates a thick "soup" of plant food that nourishes the smallest creatures in the sea. These in turn are food for fish. In this way, the phytoplankton are the foundation of life in the sea.

# Freshwater plants

Water lilies, duckweed, rushes, reeds—many plants grow in rivers and ponds. Some float on the surface of the water, while others are rooted in the mud or grow along the marshy banks.

## Freshwater habitats

Slow-moving rivers, lakes, and ponds can provide good habitats for plants so long as there is plenty of light and trees do not shade the water. Pond water is rich in nutrients, both from decaying animals and plants and from the surrounding land. The surface of the water may freeze in winter, but the icy blanket protects lower layers from the freezing air.

## Rooted in the mud

Many plants have their roots under the water but grow out into the air. Reeds grow on the edge of a pond. They are a kind of grass, and their thick stems push horizontally through the marshy ground. Water lilies grow in deeper water. The giant water lily's roots lie deep in the mud. Its long, tough stems grow to the surface and poke out into the light. The plant produces huge round leaves that are able to float on the water because of a network of supporting ribs on the underside of each leaf.

*The graceful leaves of the water lily spread across the surface of lakes and ponds, pushing other plants aside.*

## Floating on water

Some water plants are not rooted in the mud but float freely on the surface of the water. The water hyacinth is one of these. Its trailing roots take in nutrients from the water, and their weight helps to keep the plant upright. Duckweed, one of the smallest flowering plants, also floats on the surface, its single root hanging like a thread in the water. Some waterweeds grow under the water, where there is less light. They have ribbon-like stems and fine leaves that can clog up ponds.

*Water hyacinths form dense mats that float on the water's surface. These mats can create problems for fishermen and other people who rely on the water for their day-to-day activities. The mats also cause a drop in oxygen levels, which can be fatal for water animals.*

27

# Glossary

**Adaptation**
The process by which plants change in order to survive.

**Alga** (plural: algae)
A simple kind of non-flowering plant.

**Camouflage**
Coloring that helps plants or animals blend with their surroundings.

**Canopy**
The top layer of a tree or a forest, made up of leaves and branches.

**Carbon dioxide**
One of the gases in air. Plants take in carbon dioxide during photosynthesis.

**Climate zones**
Areas of the world that share the same climate.

**Conifers**
Mostly evergreen trees that grow cones and usually have needle-shaped leaves.

**Deciduous trees**
Trees or shrubs that are usually broad-leaved and lose their leaves in fall.

**Diversity**
A variety of many different kinds.

**Epiphyte**
A plant that grows on another plant and uses it for support.

**Equator**
The imaginary line around the widest part of the Earth.

**Germinate**
When a seed starts to grow.

**Habitat**
The place to which a plant is best suited and where it usually grows.

**Nutrient**
A substance that gives plants energy or helps them grow.

**Oxygen**
A gas that is found in air. Plants give out oxygen during photosynthesis.

**Photosynthesis**
The process by which plants use the energy in sunlight to turn water from the soil and carbon dioxide from the air into carbohydrates, their food.

**Pollinate**
To carry pollen from the male parts of one plant to the female parts of another.

## Reproduce
To produce offspring. A plant reproduces when it makes new plants.

## Sap
The juice inside a plant that carries food around.

## Temperate
A place or climate with moderate temperatures and four seasons in the year.

## Tropical
A place or climate that is warm throughout the year because it is near the equator.

## Web sites

**www.urbanext.uiuc.edu/gpe/index.html**
This interactive Web site looks at the different parts of plants and how they grow.

**www.mbgnet.net/**
Learn more about plant habitats where you live and around the world with this colorful and informative Web site.

**www.EnchantedLearning.com/biomes/**
Find out more about the plants and animals that live in each climate zone.

# Answers to "What's this?"

**Page 10** Blueberry

**Page 14** Edelweiss

**Page 16** Maple tree

**Page 19** Date palm

**Page 21** Baobab tree

**Page 23** Rubber tree

# Index